26 July 1995

W9-CRT-258

Bel Canto:
A Theoretical & Practical Vocal Method

Mathilde Marchesi

with a new introduction by

PHILIP L. MILLER

FORMER CHIEF OF THE MUSIC DIVISION, NEW YORK PUBLIC LIBRARY

Dover Publications, Inc., New York

To my dear daughter, Blanche Marchesi

Published in Canada by General Publishing Company, Ltd., 30 Lesmill Road, Don Mills, Toronto, Ontario.
Published in the United Kingdom by Constable and Company, Ltd., 10 Orange Street, London WC 2.

This Dover edition, first published in 1970, is an unabridged republication of the work originally published by Enoch & Sons, Ltd., London, n.d. A new introduction has been written for the present edition by Philip L. Miller.

International Standard Book Number: 0-486-22315-9
Library of Congress Catalog Card Number: 79-116817

Manufactured in the United States of America
Dover Publications, Inc.
180 Varick Street
New York, N.Y. 10014

INTRODUCTION TO THE DOVER EDITION

One day in 1886 a young Australian named Mrs. Mitchell made an appointment to sing for the great Mme. Marchesi in Paris. She had come up to London not long before, had given a recital in Princes' Hall, which the critic Herman Klein later remembered as "decidedly amateurish and mediocre," and had sung for Sir Arthur Sullivan, whose best encouragement was that after a year's study he *might* be able to offer her a role in *The Mikado*. Marchesi's reaction was different. "Salvatore!" she called to her husband, "at last I have found a star." She then assured the young woman, "If you are serious and can study with me for one year, I can make something extraordinary of you." As everyone knows, the debut of Nellie Melba in *Rigoletto* at the Théâtre de la Monnaie in Brussels, 12 October 1887, was indeed extraordinary, for it launched one of the most sensational musical careers of all time. Melba's studies with Marchesi did not stop with her debut; she never lost contact until the end of the teacher's life. By that time her own name was a long established household word. Her career finally reached its end in a historic farewell at Covent Garden, 8 June 1926. She was then just past her sixty-fifth birthday—or her sixty-seventh, according to which biographical dictionary you read.

The reason for recalling this is to point out one of the differences between the life and longevity of a prima donna over the turn of the century and at the present time. In Melba's day one year was an unusually short time to spend preparing for a debut, which fact indicates that her voice must have been naturally produced to begin with. It was normal for an aspirant to go to a master and stay until he was pronounced ready, were it two years or six. Nowadays, with our accelerated way of life, our rapid travel and our eagerness to live while we are young, it is a rare singer who has that kind of patience. At the same time, audiences are less tolerant of ungainly figures on the stage; in this day of the producer, opera must be credible drama, unfortunately often first and foremost.

There never was a time when connoisseurs of singing did not lament the passing of a "golden age," a period when vocalists really knew how to sing. Today we have recordings to demonstrate the ways in which older singers differed from those now active, though we should never forget (as many enthusiasts do) that

the art and science of recording in 1906 was a very different thing from what we know today. There are those who praise the past to the extent that they can concede nothing good to the present; and there are those who can hear nothing but scratch in the old recordings.

Until the introduction of the microphone into the studio in 1925, that is, until the advent of electrical recording, singers were divided into two classes—those who "took" well and those who did not. Singing into the huge acoustical horn was an ordeal at best. Some could accustom themselves to it, some could not. But of one thing we can always be sure: if a singer sounds well on an acoustic record, we know he must have sounded even better in real life. And we can hear enough, even in the more primitive old discs, to recognize schools and methods of singing. There is something common to the recorded voices of Melba, Calvé, Eames and Alda—all Marchesi pupils—indeed, we can hear this something even in the very early (and very rare) discs of Frances Saville. They all have a solidity, a sure technical mastery, an even scale with no register break. Their trills are strong, even and secure, their coloratura masterly. It is an oversimplification to say they sang "instrumentally": Calvé was renowned for her coloring of the words she sang, and we can detect something of this approach in the records of Eames.

It will be noted in the story of Melba's audition that Mme. Marchesi not only knew how to develop a voice; she could spot exceptional talent when she came on it. If she had not chosen her pupils with the greatest care it is doubtful that she would have had so many great singers to her credit. She taught only women, and mostly sopranos—though the Australian contralto Ada Crossley (whose records are very early and rare) came to her after she had already had some experience.

Mme. Marchesi was born Mathilde Graumann in Frankfurt am Main 24 March 1821. It was only after the failure of the family fortunes that she went, at the age of twenty-two, to Vienna for study with Nicolai, later journeying to Paris to work with the younger Manuel Garcia. She remained with him four years. For a time she served as his assistant, and during a period when he was incapacitated she took over his classes. Thus she laid the foundations of her own lifework. In 1852 she married Salvatore Marchesi, himself a baritone and a teacher, with whom she had something of an opera and concert career. After a period in London she returned to Vienna as professor at the conservatory, then back to Paris, to Cologne and Vienna, finally settling in Paris in 1881. She died in London 17 November 1913.

It has been said that the "Marchesi Method" died with its founder; certainly the most assiduous study of her writings and her vocalises will not reveal all the secrets of her teaching. But with the present-day interest in the "bel canto" operas of Rossini, Donizetti and Bellini and the ever growing public enthusiasm for the Mozart masterpieces, there is a need for great vocalism. The serious artist will not be satisfied with "instant" methods and general corner-cutting. And so we turn to the exercises, the precepts and the recordings of an earlier day.

Mme. Marchesi's ground rules are simple enough. She insisted on the analytical method of study; exercises and scales must never be sung mechanically. "The pupil," she says, "should, from the very first lesson, cultivate a habit of analysing, or mentally preparing, the exercises &c., before commencing to sing them." She used to tell her students to listen to the orchestra and approximate the sound of each instrument as it accompanied the voice. She believed in the importance of correct breathing: "Normal respiration, or the natural breathing of a healthy person, is *diaphragmatic* or *abdominal*." She described the stroke of the glottis as "a natural movement of the vocal organs," and declared that the pupil "has only to bring under the control of the will this spontaneous action which has been developing since the first cry at the moment of birth." She warned against too much practice: "The least excess in practising causes exhaustion." The beginning pupil should limit himself to five or ten consecutive minutes, but such periods may be repeated three or four times a day. Gradually the five minutes may be increased to a half hour. At this point it may be of interest to recall a statement by Melba: "During the development of the average voice, scales and

solfeggios and vocalization over its entire range are absolutely essential to its proper growth; but once the period of vocal maturity is reached, I am sure all students who sing in public will be wise to reserve their voices as much as possible in private."

Perhaps a key to Marchesi's success may be found in this statement: "Pupils should never be burdened with more than one difficulty at a time, and they should be assisted in overcoming obstacles by having them presented in a natural and progressive order." A teacher should pass on to singing with words only when the pupil's voice is perfectly placed throughout its entire compass, when the three registers are completely blended, and when the vocal organ has acquired a sufficient degree of ease and flexibility. But lest it be understood from this that hers was a strictly "instrumental" method, unconcerned with the text, she once wrote: "A singer with a moderately good voice, who has mastered the significance of his words, will always have the advantage over the possessor of a much finer instrument to whom they are a sealed message. Gounod was wont to say of a singer of the latter type, 'What a beautiful organ pipe.'"

But even in Marchesi's day there was a growing tendency to look for quick and easy methods. W. J. Henderson, writing a preface for one of Marchesi's books, says, "There is not now in Europe a single school in which six years are given to the mechanical part of singing." Further: "Madame Marchesi did not find four years too long for the pursuit of her studies with this master [Garcia], who would have found a short road to the art of singing if there had been one." Even in those days one might smile at the eighteenth-century story of Porpora dismissing his pupil Cafarelli as ready for a career after working seven years on one sheet of vocalises. But it seems clear that with Marchesi one would have worked on each exercise until it was mastered and then have passed on to the next. One could not be sure what this would mean in time. The method certainly produced an impressive number of great singers.

PHILIP L. MILLER

PREFACE.

———◆———

THE *Theoretical and Practical Vocal Method* that I now publish is an educational work which commences with the vocal alphabet, that is to say, with elementary exercises, and contains also a series of *Elementary and Progressive Vocalises* for the formation of the mechanism of the voice.

I would again set forth the principle that I have already laid down in prefaces to different works that I have published, which is, that in order to obtain a speedy and satisfactory result, pupils should never be burdened with more than one difficulty at a time, and they should be assisted in overcoming obstacles by having them presented in a natural and progressive order. It is with this object in view that I have written special Exercises and Vocalises for each particular difficulty.

It is essential that the mechanism of the voice should be trained to execute all possible rhythmical and musical forms before passing to the æsthetical part of the art of singing.

May this work, which I look upon as my last of the kind, add to the important results that I have obtained from forty-two years' application of my system.

MATHILDE MARCHESI.

CONTENTS.

FIRST PART.

ELEMENTARY AND PROGRESSIVE EXERCISES FOR THE DEVELOPMENT OF THE VOICE.

SECOND PART.

DEVELOPMENT OF THE EXERCISES IN THE FORM OF VOCALISES.

PRACTICAL GUIDE FOR STUDENTS.

ATTITUDE OF THE SINGER.

THE attitude of the pupil, in singing, should be as natural and easy as possible. The body should be kept upright, the head erect, the shoulders well thrown back, without effort, and the chest free. In order to give perfect freedom to the vocal organs whilst singing, all the muscles surrounding those parts should be completely relaxed.

THE MOUTH.

As the vocal tube extends to the lips, the beauty of a voice may be quite spoilt by a faulty position of the mouth.

The smiling mouth, for example, favoured by many professors past and present, is absurd, and quite contrary to the laws of acoustics. Smiling causes the mouth to assume the position required for pronouncing the Italian vowel E (pronounced *ay*). This vowel makes the vocal tube square, and gives a too open tone to the voice, called by the Italians *voce sgangherata* and by the French *voix blanche*. Therefore, the mouth should be opened naturally, by letting the chin fall, as in pronouncing " ah " (not too broad), and it must be kept immovable in this position for the entire duration of the sound.

In opening the mouth, only the lower jaw moves, the upper one is fixed ; hence the necessity for lowering the chin. The muscles of the jaw possess great contractile power (indispensable for mastication), and will not, at first, remain relaxed during the whole length of the sound, but with practice they will eventually gain the necessary elasticity. When this elasticity is once acquired, it will enable the chin to articulate the consonants distinctly and rapidly in singing.

RESPIRATION.

Respiration consists of *Inspiration*, during which the air passes through the glottis, the trachea or windpipe, and the bronchial tubes to enter the lungs ; and of *Expiration*, during which the air is breathed out again through the same channels.

In the normal state, these two movements succeed one another in a regular and rhythmical manner and *without any intervention of the will, as during sleep*. Consequently, all premeditated action for facilitating or regulating these functions in a special manner is fatally injurious, because it opposes and impairs the freedom of the normal movements of the vocal organs and of the muscles which govern them. In addition to the outward movement of the ribs, the chest (thorax, a bony, conical cage, slightly flattened) can expand, in *Inspiration*, at its base, summit, and sides. So there are *three* respiratory movements, or three kinds of breathing, namely :—

Diaphragmatic or *Abdominal* ;
Clavicular ;
Lateral or Intercostal.

The lungs, formed of a spongy, elastic tissue, perforated in every part by thousands of little tubes destined to receive the air, are concave and largest at their base, and separated from the abdominal cavity by a convex muscular partition, called the Diaphragm, upon which they rest. At the moment of *Inspiration* this partition descends, causing the base of the lungs to expand.

Normal respiration, or the natural breathing of a healthy person, is *diaphragmatic* or *abdominal*. By this method of respiration the lungs are expanded at the base, and consequently receive the greatest quantity of air. By the other methods, which are bad, the lungs are only partly filled; whence the necessity for more frequent breathing and the impossibility of singing long phrases in a single breath.

The use of the corset by females causes *lateral* breathing, because it compresses the abdominal walls. Ladies who would become singers are, therefore, strongly advised to avoid clothes which, by interfering with the freedom of the waist, prevent the inflation of the lungs at the base.

ATTACK.—COUP DE GLOTTE.

After the lungs are filled, it is necessary, for the production of a sound, that the pupil should hermetically close the glottis so that its extreme edges, called the *Vocal Cords*, may be set vibrating by the air which bursts through at the moment of *Expiration*. The *Coup de Glotte* requires, then, a sudden and energetic approximation of the lips of the *glottis*, an instant before *Expiration* commences.

This organic action, which forms the *Attack* or *Emission* of the voice, is brought about by preparing the glottis and mouth for the production of a vowel. As stated above, the best vowel to use for the formation and development of the voice is the Italian vowel A (*ah*), attacking it naturally and without effort or affectation.

It should be understood that the *Coup de Glotte* is a natural movement of the vocal organs, and that the pupil has only to bring under the control of the will this spontaneous action which has been developing since the first cry at the moment of birth. It is, in fact, the possession of this same natural faculty that enables us to form unconsciously all the vowels in speaking.

The closing of the glottis is, then, a natural and spontaneous organic action. But, in speaking, this action is intermittent, the opening of the lips of the glottis being followed by their contraction with an equal rapidity. The pupil need do no more than endeavour to keep the glottis contracted after its lips have been brought together. That is to say, when once the note has been attacked, it is necessary to practise holding the glottis contracted as long as the professor considers it expedient for the development of the elasticity of the vocal organs, development which practice will increase daily. We repeat, then, that if the pupil would acquire a good attack, the glottis must be closed an instant before *Expiration* commences; in other words, it should be prepared.

If the column of air issuing from the lungs finds the glottis open, and, in consequence of there being no obstacle in its way, no body is set vibrating, then the result is *Aphony* (no sound). If the *Vocal Cords* are not firmly and evenly closed throughout their entire extent at the instant that the air commences to escape from the lungs, the lips of the glottis being unable to fully contract during *Expiration*, the sound will be weak and hoarse, and the intonation uncertain, because the *Vocal Cords* do not vibrate throughout their entire extent, and the vibrations cannot be isochronous (equal). Moreover, because the air escapes in puffs and the lungs empty rapidly, the sound is of short duration, and the pupil's respiration is short and unsteady, as the supply of breath has to be renewed so frequently.

To sum up, the firmer and more complete the approximation of the lips of the glottis, the more resistance they will offer to the air which escapes from the lungs, and the less air it will take to set the *Vocal Cords* vibrating. The slower the *Expiration*, the longer the sound will last. The equal and continuous pressure of the air against the vibrating body produces *isochronous* (equal) vibrations, and maintains equality of sound throughout its entire duration.

REGISTERS OF THE FEMALE VOICE.

This is the *Alpha* and *Omega* of the formation and development of the female voice, the touchstone of all singing methods, old and new. As this is to be, above all, a *Practical Guide* for students, this important subject cannot here be treated in detail. The anatomical, physiological, and acoustical explanations and demonstrations necessary for a clear understanding of the organic phenomena which cause the three series of consecutive and homogeneous sounds of the three registers, of an essentially different nature, I give verbally to pupils, with the aid of anatomical charts and an artificial human larynx.

Nevertheless, before offering any practical remarks upon this subject, so important in the formation of the voice, I consider it necessary to explain, in a few words, the production of sound in general, in order to make clear to the pupil the theory which establishes the existence of the three registers. Moreover, as all the sounds belonging to one register are of the same nature, the modifications of intensity and quality which they can undergo are of little moment.

Sound is a property of the air, as colour is of light, for there can be no sound without air, any more than there can be colour without light. At the present day, the immediate causes of effects in these great phenomena of nature are well known, but the principles underlying these causes are yet to be discovered. The special organization, interior and exterior, of a body, which by its oscillations sets the air vibrating, or by its surface reflects light in a particular manner, decides the nature of the sound or of the shade of the colour.

Three things are needed for the production of a sound, viz. : a *Motor*, which acts either by sending a column of air against a vibrating body, or by immediate friction with this body ; a *Vibrator*, which executes a certain number of regular (isochronous) or irregular vibrations in a given time when set in motion by the *Motor ;* and, finally, a *Resonator* (because of its function, it would be more correct to call it the co-operating element), which receives the sounding column of air that escapes from the vibrating body to imbue it with the character of its own sound by reverberation. These three elements, indispensable for the production of sound, are found in all wind, stringed, or percussion instruments. It is, therefore, only logical to admit that they should also exist in the vocal organs.

Upon examination, it will be found that the tone of all these instruments is of a similar nature throughout the entire compass, and that they are free from those sudden changes in the quality of the sound that are met with in the human voice. This is because the three generating elements of sound, in these instruments, are unalterable in their functions as well as in their shapes and sizes.

If we examine these three elements in the vocal organs, we find that the *Motor* (the lungs and the parts connected with them) may possess greater or lesser activity, more or less power and elasticity, according to its physiological or pathological state, but the nature of its functions never changes, neither does its organic form alter. The *Vibrator* (the glottis) in its normal state is susceptible of innumerable degrees of tension and contraction, but it is unalterable in its function. The glottis can, indeed, augment or diminish the intensity of the sound, by a corresponding increase or decrease in the number of vibrations of the *Vocal Cords*, according to the force of the concussion caused by the air in *Expiration ;* it can also raise or lower the pitch, by shortening or lengthening the *Vocal Cords*, in combination with the modifications of the shape of the resonance tube, but no alteration can be discovered in its functional activity as a *Vibrating body* that would account for the different nature of the sound in the change of registers. It is evident, therefore, that the secret of the phenomenon met with in passing from one register to another is to be found in the *Resonator* of the vocal organs. It is the *Larynx* which, by change of position, directs the column of air escaping from the *Vibrator* (the glottis) towards the three resonant walls alternately.

Since, then, each register of the voice consists of a series of consecutive and homogeneous sounds, of an essentially different kind to those of the other registers, it follows that the vocal apparatus should contain three quite distinct resonance chambers (walls). These three *Resonators*, formed of different organic tissues, impart, by reason of their special physiological properties, a distinct character to each series of sounds contained within the limits of each register.

After many years' successful experience, I am convinced that scientific knowledge is indispensable to professors of singing, because it enables them to treat the vocal instrument in a natural and rational manner and with greater certainty; also, by showing them the causes of the defects, it helps them in training difficult voices and in correcting the numerous faults of emission that each pupil brings, the result either of bad habits or inferior training.

If we do not teach the elements of the anatomy and physiology of the human voice, we needlessly deprive the pupil of the means of becoming acquainted with the physical phenomena of the vocal organs. Each pupil should, therefore, at least be taught how to manage and preserve the voice in its career, and should understand the exact meaning of the words *Larynx, Glottis, Vocal Cords,* &c., words which the antagonists of the physiology of the voice are themselves obliged to use continually in speaking of the art of singing.

I most emphatically maintain that the female voice possesses *three* registers, and not *two*, and I strongly impress upon my pupils this undeniable fact, which, moreover, their own experience teaches them, after a few lessons.

The three registers of the female voice are the **Chest**, the *Medium*, and the *Head.* I use the term *Medium* and not *Falsetto* (the word used for the middle register by some professors of singing), firstly, because the word *Medium* (middle) precisely and logically explains the position that this register occupies in the compass of the voice, and, secondly, to avoid all confusion that might be caused by the term *Falsetto*, which belongs exclusively to men's voices. *Falsetto*, which signifies *Falso* (false), that is, *in place of the true*, is a term that has been used in Italy from the earliest period in the history of the art of singing, to indicate certain *piano* effects in the high notes of the Tenor voice.

Empiricism, which in these days appears to struggle more than ever against the incessant progress made by all the sciences connected with the phenomena of the voice, as well as against all rules of modern pedagogy, has put in circulation, among other absurdities, the assertion that the female voice only possesses *two* registers, viz. : Chest and Falsetto. This grave error has also been endorsed by several eminent modern physiologists, who have persuaded themselves that they have established this theory, after their observations with the laryngoscope, but who are incapable of making comparative experiments with their own vocal organs.

Nevertheless, the female voice most certainly does possess *three* registers. But for defining the special nature of the sound of each of them, for determining their respective limits, and for blending the three registers and establishing homogeneity of sound throughout the compass of the voice, theoretical and practical knowledge is needed.

Unfortunately, it is owing to this ignorance of the limits and the treatment of these three registers of the female voice that there are so many imperfectly-trained singers, who struggle against the faults and difficulties of a mechanism wrongly used, and so many unequal voices, which possess sets of weak and heterogeneous sounds, commonly called *breaks.* These *breaks*, however, are only sounds wrongly placed and produced.

When commencing to study, the lowest notes of a register, in most voices, have not so much power as the highest notes of the preceding register. The theoretical and practical explanation that I give to pupils of this phenomenon soon convinces them that here lie difficulties, inherent to the physical construction of the vocal organs, which are easily conquered when the causes are understood. Therefore, in using the exercises designed for developing in the Larynx or Glottis those faculties that are necessary for removing this imperfection of the vocal compass, the homogeneity in the nature of the sound throughout the particular compass of each register, as well as the blending of the three registers, depends, above all, upon the ability of the professor, the patience and assiduity of the pupil, and the method of practising.

Female voices are divided into: *Contralto, Mezzo-Soprano, Dramatic Soprano,* and *Light Soprano* (sfogato). The highest note in the chest register of all female voices varies between the notes

Contralto and Mezzo-Soprano differ from Soprano voices in having generally a chest register of much greater compass, which extends more or less to the lower sounds.

To equalize and blend the *Chest* with the *Medium* register, the pupil must slightly close the two last notes of the former in ascending, and open them in descending. Every effort expended upon the highest notes of a register increases the difficulty of developing the power of the lower notes in the next register, and therefore of blending the two registers, until eventually it becomes impossible.

When the limits of the register are not fixed, there are always a series of sounds that are uncertain, weak, and out of tune, when singing a scale with full voice or a sustained phrase. According to modern pitch, the highest *chest* note of nearly all Contralto and Mezzo-Soprano voices varies from Soprano voices from

There are *Contralto* voices which, by reason of an exceptional position of the Larynx, never succeed in developing a *Head* voice. These *short* voices, which consist merely of the *Chest* and *Medium* registers, are very rare, and they can only aspire to a career as concert singers.

The limit of the *Medium* register in all female voices varies from , as a general rule, however, should be looked upon as the highest note.

As the Head voice is very rarely used for speaking in ordinary circumstances, the sounds of this register are but little developed, and, in commencing the study of singing, they present a great contrast, in intensity and volume, to the highest notes of the *Medium* register. More time is needed, therefore, for the development of the *Head* register than for the other registers.

The same instructions that we have given for the change and blending of the *Chest* and *Medium* registers apply also to those of the *Medium* and *Head*.

METHOD OF STUDY.

A rational and progressive course of vocal gymnastics will develop great elasticity as well as a great power of contraction in the muscles of the vocal organs, without ever causing fatigue; whilst the least excess in practising causes exhaustion. In commencing study, the pupil should not continue singing too long at the time, and, at first, the practice should not last longer than five or ten minutes, repeated, after long intervals, three or four times a day. The time devoted to practice may be gradually increased five minutes at the time to half an hour. A conscientious professor will never allow the lesson to last longer than half an hour.

If, as very frequently happens, the pupil disregards these instructions and practises at home longer than the professor advises, that distressing result, fatigue of the voice, will soon follow. In this case the *Vocal Cords*, the most delicate and important part of the vocal organs, are the first to be affected, and it will be necessary to stop the practice for a time. This interruption of study, at the beginning, is sufficient to undo all the work that had already been done. Besides the loss of precious time, the pupil has also to regret the loss of the progress that has been made by the muscles of the vocal organs. It is of the greatest importance that the pupil should always commence, when practising at home, with the emission of the voice, and continue the exercises in the order appointed by the professor. In order to develop the power, extent, and equality of the voice, and to succeed in blending the registers, the scales should be practised with full voice, but without forcing it, and avoiding shouting.

ANALYSIS.

The greater number of pupils who learn singing have very little knowledge of music. They commence, consequently, by singing the exercises and scales mechanically, guided entirely by the ear, paying no attention to the length and rhythmical division of each bar, or the particular value of each note. This method of singing by ear is most pernicious, and wastes much of the pupil's time ; besides, when studying in this manner, the pupil is obliged to repeat the same passage over and over again, which, instead of aiding the progress, only tends to tire the vocal organs. Therefore, the pupil should, from the very first lesson, cultivate a habit of analysing, or mentally preparing, the exercises, &c., before commencing to sing them. It is only by finding out the exact motive of the task in hand that pupils can so grasp the ideas of the professor as to make them guide their studies and lead on to the road of independence.

If this analytical method is adopted by the pupil from the very beginning, it will be of great assistance in all the different periods of study, as well as in his or her professional career, when new works have to be studied. It will also prove of great service when, in passing to the second part of my method (the Elementary and Graduated Vocalises), new difficulties are encountered, such as the different kinds of time (duple, triple, &c.), the various modulations, the multiform divisions of each bar, the very varied rhythmical accents, and, finally, the new combinations of intervals constantly occurring.

When the time, the division of each bar, and the accentuation of the phrase are understood, the pupil may commence to sing with full voice, because then the attention need only be given to the intonation, and a successful result will be obtained before fatigue sets in.

After finishing the course of Vocalises, the pupil should pass on to the third part of my Method, which contains Vocalises with words, and where still further purely mechanical difficulties will be found.

In accordance with my system, explained in the Preface to this work, which consists of presenting to the pupil only a single obstacle at a time, I have composed Vocalises with words, for blending pronunciation with vocalization ; that is to say, for accustoming the pupil to pronounce the words distinctly, without affecting the emission of the voice, and not neglecting to correct the faults of pronunciation ; and this should be done before commencing to sing Airs, and before giving thought to the sentiment or expression. For this purpose I have chosen the Italian language, because it is the only one that is free from the guttural vowels of Teutonic languages, and the closed and nasal ones of the French language ; without mentioning certain consonants produced by the root of the tongue in the former languages, or the " *grasseyement* "* generally met with among the French.

---

* " Grasseyement," defective pronunciation of the letter R.

It is impossible to give rules for correcting the very many faults of pronunciation that one meets with in pupils. They must be left to the skill and experience of the professor. Not only do these faults of pronunciation of the various nationalities differ among themselves, but they vary very considerably even among pupils of the same country, being the result either of a special organization, bad habits, or the particular dialect spoken in each of the provincial towns of the different countries.

Equality in the emission of sound upon the five simple Italian vowels *a, e, i, o, u;* the correction of defective articulation of the consonants by the means best adapted to each individual; and the formation of a habit of good pronunciation—these are the tasks for the pupil commencing the third part of my Method.

The closed E and O, that one would willingly receive into the Italian language, do not, however, exist in it, although the sentiment, sad or cheerful, of a word or a phrase impels the orator, actor, or singer to close or open the vowels. So, too, words are frequently met with that express alternatively grief and terror, or joy and sarcasm.

In order to properly render the sense of the situation, it is necessary, therefore, to close or open the vowel of a word in accordance with the sentiment to be expressed. As to the consonants, it is the linguals *l, d, t, s, z, r, n, c, g, k, q, x,* that interfere with the emission of the sound when commencing to sing words, because the root of the tongue is so closely attached to the larynx. They alter the equilibrium of the tension and the regularity of the vibrations of the vocal cords, because the movements of the tongue jerk the larynx. After a time, practice will render these movements independent of the operations of the larynx.

The pupil should look upon the studies in the third part as belonging exclusively to the mechanism of the art of singing, since expression or sentiment has yet to be dealt with. Nevertheless, as the different melodies have been inspired by the sense of the words, they commence to develop the taste and sentiment of the pupil in regard to phrasing and style.

In commencing this part of my Method, pupils who have hitherto followed the system of analysis adopted at the beginning of their studies will be quite competent to decipher the musical part of the *Vocalises with words,* by reading them, at first, without the text, in the manner indicated above. The next thing to do, before commencing to sing the *Vocalises,* is to distribute the syllables to their notes.

When once a complete mastery has been obtained over the mechanism of the voice, as well as over all the degrees of power, expression, and of quality and colour of sound that the vocal organs can produce, and when the movements of the tongue and lips are thoroughly under control, then the pupil can easily learn to sing in any language, without sacrificing beauty of sound to clear pronunciation of each syllable, or distinct pronunciation to beauty of sound.

When all mechanical difficulties have been overcome, from the formation of sound up to pronunciation, the pupil may pass on to the study of the Air with Recitative, and so enter upon the æsthetics of the art of singing without being arrested every moment by vocal or musical faults, or by a badly pronounced word or syllable. Pupils can now give their attention exclusively to the sentiment and expression, and commence to acquire a knowledge of the different styles found in the many kinds of vocal music.

In studying an Air, pupils should always employ the same analytical system they have used hitherto. They should commence, therefore, by reading and translating the text, trying to get an idea of the character they have to represent, studying, at the same time, the dramatic situation in which this character is placed at the moment of singing the particular Air. At this psychological moment, so important for the development of the sentiment and mode of expression, the pupil should obtain from the professor every explanation that can facilitate the task.

Later on, when the studies in singing, elocution, and acting have come to an end, and pupils in the course of their careers as singers are called upon to learn new works, they will find that this system of analysing the measure, text, character, and dramatic situation, before commencing to sing, will give them a great advantage over other vocalists. Both voice and time will be saved, and the spirit of a new piece or *rôle* will be more quickly seized by them than by others.

STYLE.

People frequently speak of the Italian, French, or German *School* or *Style* of singing. Having resided for many years in the different centres of these three nationalities, I can safely say that, with the exception of national songs of a popular and local character, peculiar to each nation, there are only two Vocal Schools in the whole world: the *good*, from which the best results are obtained, and the *bad*, in which the reverse is the case. The same may be said with regard to style. It is, therefore, quite a mistake to speak of a German, English, French, or Italian Vocal School or Style.

There have always been many great singers of both sexes belonging to different European nations who have been received with the same degree of enthusiasm at Paris as at Rome, London, St. Petersburg, &c.

Before bringing this *Practical Guide* to conclusion, I must again call the attention of pupils to a serious error, disseminated in these days by empiricism. It is argued, that because modern vocal music consists of long and declaimed phrases, without florid passages or embellishments, it is unnecessary (so it is said) for the singer to cultivate the mechanism of the voice, as it tires the vocal organs and causes loss of time to the pupil.

As regards the fatigue of the vocal organs caused by practice, that depends entirely upon the ability of the professor and the intelligent docility of the pupil. As to all that concerns the technical requirements of the long and declaimed phrases of modern vocal music, the true facts are quite at variance with these statements.

A singer who has learnt how to breathe well, and who has equalized the voice, neatly blended the registers, and developed the activity of the larynx and the elasticity of the glottis and resonant tube in a rational manner, so that all possible shades of tone, power, and expression can be produced by the vocal organs, would most assuredly be able to sing well, and without fatigue or effort (that is, without exaggeration or shouting), the long and declaimed modern phrases. While a singer whose respiration is badly managed, and who lacks control over the vocal organs, and, consequently, exaggerates and distorts the modern musical phrase, will very soon tire the voice.

Every art consists of a technical-mechanical part and an æsthetical part. A singer who cannot overcome the difficulties of the first part can never attain perfection in the second, not even a genius.

THE MARCHESI VOCAL METHOD.

FIRST PART.

ELEMENTARY AND PROGRESSIVE EXERCISES FOR THE DEVELOPMENT OF THE VOICE.

EMISSION OF THE VOICE.

OPEN the mouth naturally, keep it quite still, and draw in breath slowly; then attack the sounds neatly on the broad Italian vowel A (*ah*), by a resolute articulation or stroke of the glottis (*coup de glotte*) avoiding all jerkiness as well as effort.

2

CHROMATIC SLUR.

DIATONIC SLUR.

PORTAMENTO.

E. & S. 2326.

PORTAMENTO.

SCALES.

The voice in its natural state is as a rule rough, uneven, heavy, and of limited compass. Having secured accuracy of intonation in the attack of each sound (by the stroke of the glottis) the next task should be the development of volume, power, and compass of the voice, and the blending of the registers. The pupil should not at first attempt to sing the complete scale, but begin by practising exercises of two three and four notes, etc., otherwise there is a risk of never succeeding in any kind of passage.

All scales should be transposed throughout the compass of the voice a semitone at a time up and down, care being taken not to over-exert the extreme limits of the voice; they should be sung with perfect equality of length and power as well as with correct intonation of the half tones. When the descending scale is out of tune it is because the semitones are too wide.

All scales and exercises should be sung with full voice but without forcing.   By practising with half voice (*mezza voce*) the tension of the glottis will never develop, neither will the sound attain the requisite power.   The pupil is advised not to practise more than a quarter of an hour at a time.   It is left to the teacher to extend this period when the pupil is sufficiently advanced

N.B.—All scales and exercises to be transposed into the keys best adapted to each voice.

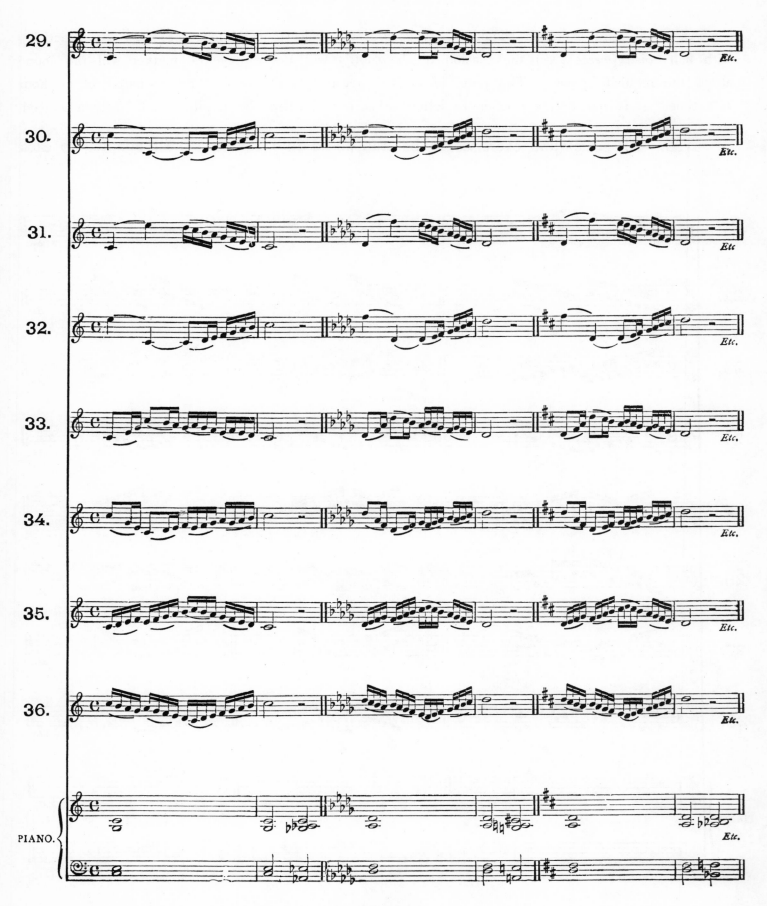

EXERCISES FOR BLENDING THE REGISTERS.
CHROMATIC THIRD.

To be transposed into other keys.*

* It is left to the teacher to decide which scales and exercises are best adapted to the capacity and voice of the pupil

E. & S. 2328.

12

All scales should be sung slowly at first, taking breath after each bar, so that the voice may be well developed and equalized. The proper method of breathing is to stop after the first note of any bar, take breath during its remaining beats, and then start with the note just quitted, at the beginning of a fresh bar (see example below.)*

When the pupil is more advanced the speed may be increased and two or more bars taken in one breath.

14

46.

47.

PIANO.

⊕ EXAMPLE.   Take breath.

46   En.

16

E. & S. 2328.

56.

57.

PIANO.

The scales from Nos. 60 to 67 are especially intended for light Soprani; they should not be attempted until the voice has attained a certain degree of flexibility.

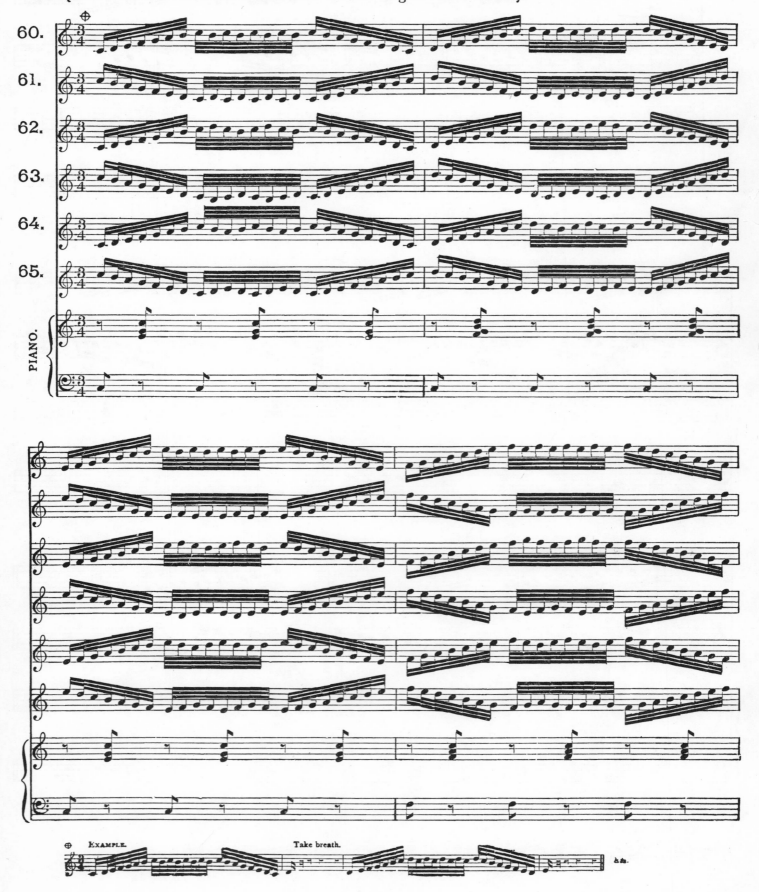

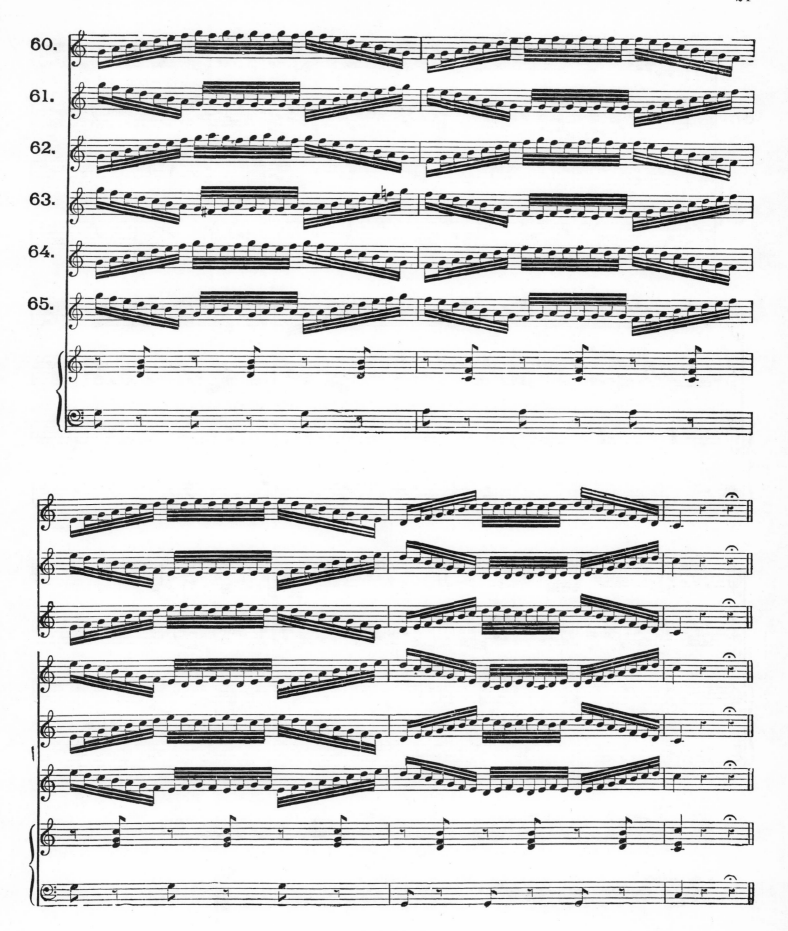

23

E. & S. 2328.

The exercises on two, three, four, six, and eight notes, are useful for blending the registers, increasing flexibility, and for accuracy of intonation. Like the scales, they must be sung slowly at first, breathing at intervals, and transposing them a semitone at a time, higher or lower, to suit the voice. As in the scales the speed may be increased and the frequent breathing omitted when the pupil is sufficiently advanced.

EXERCISES ON TWO NOTES.

EXERCISES ON THREE NOTES.

EXERCISES ON FOUR NOTES.

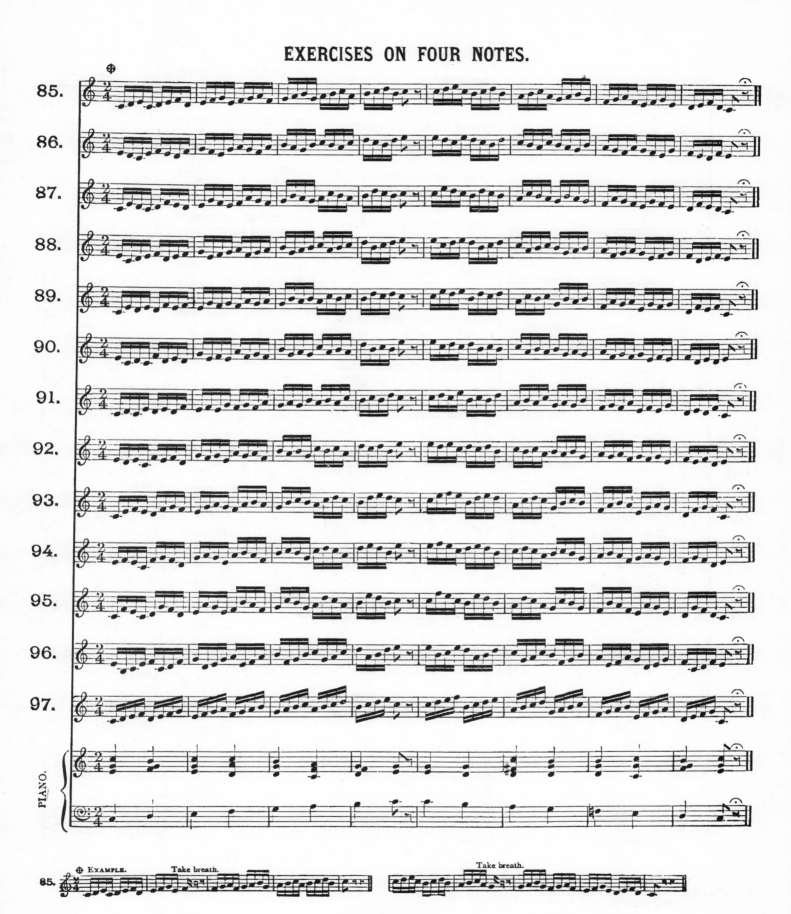

EXERCISES ON SIX NOTES.

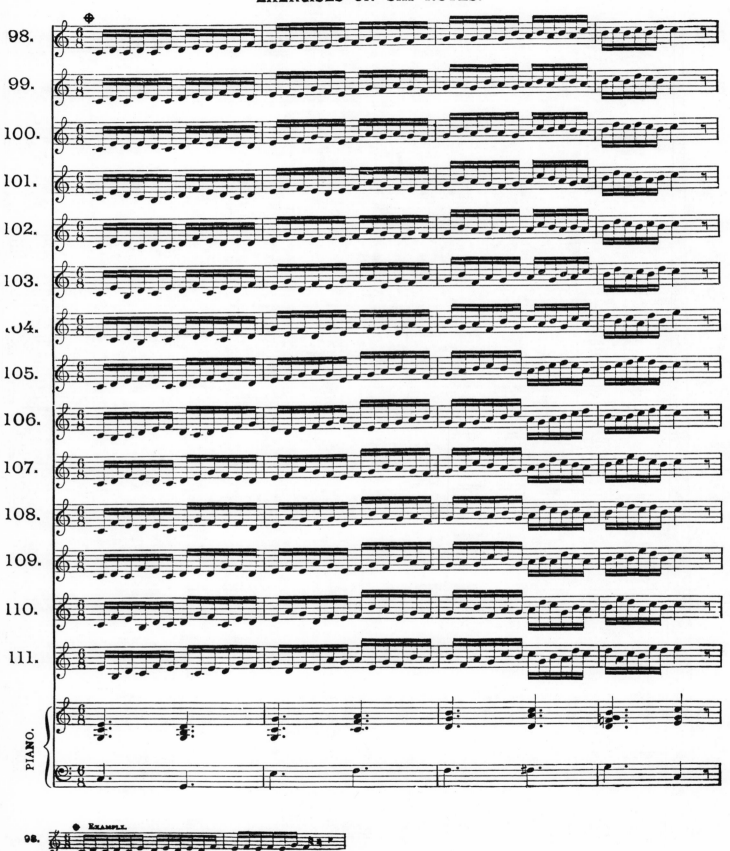

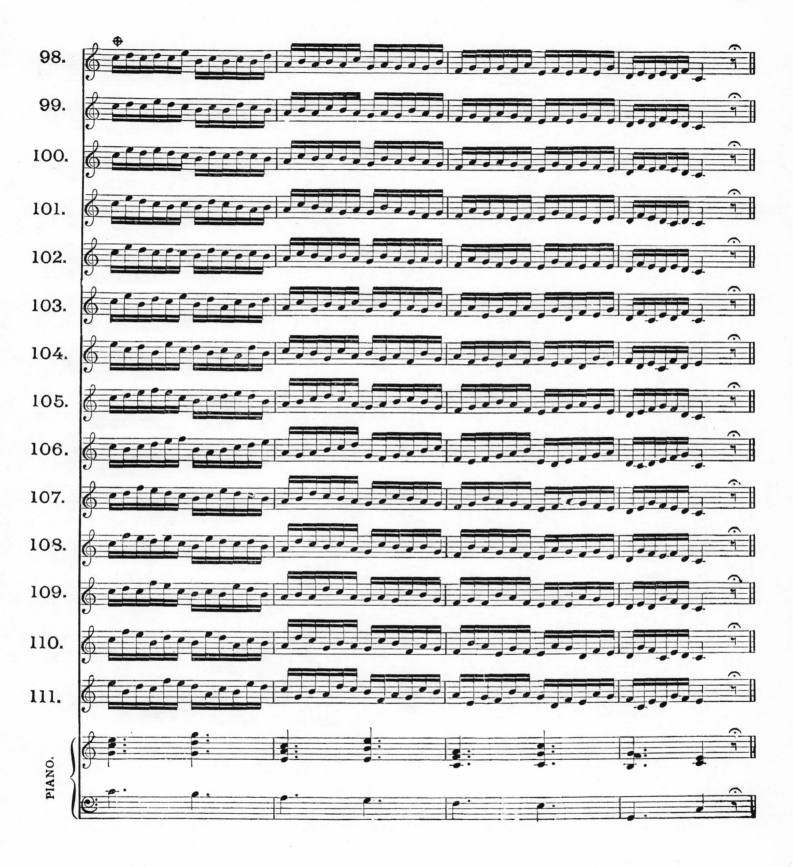

EXERCISES ON EIGHT NOTES.

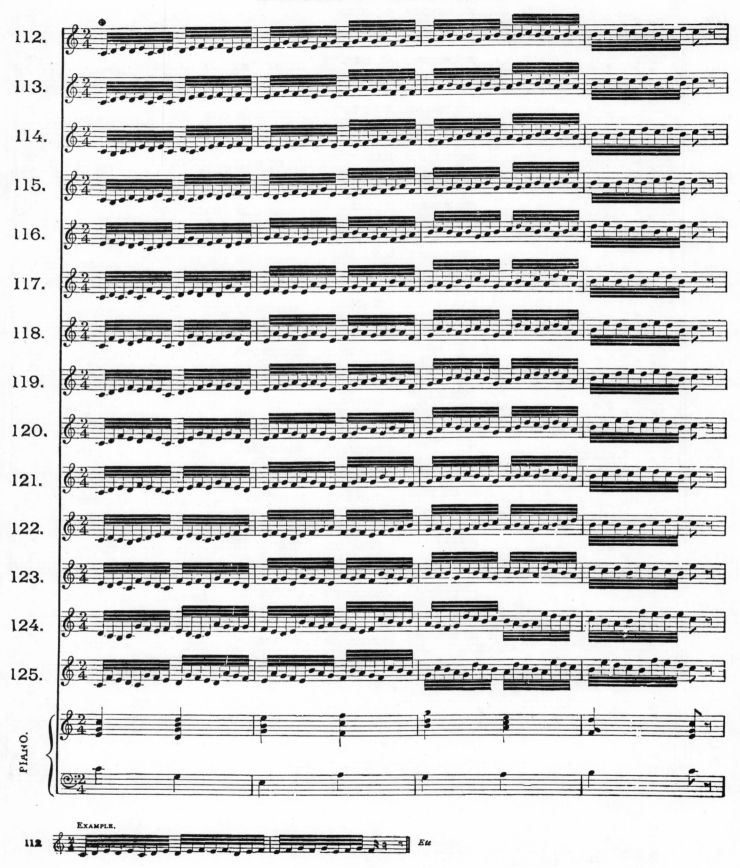

EXAMPLE.

112.   Etc

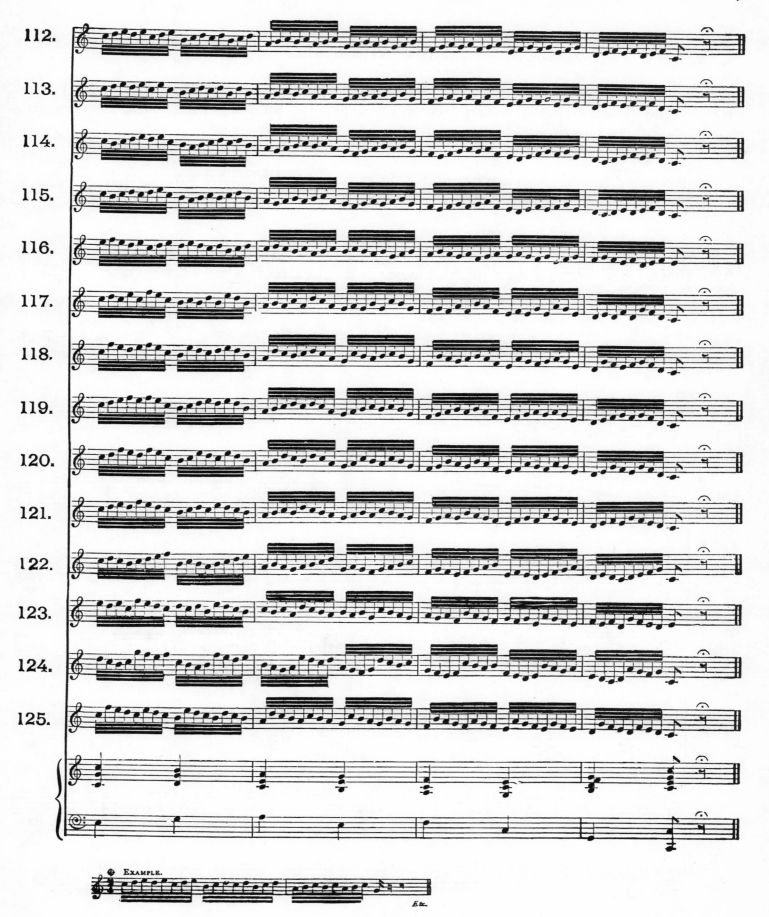

CHROMATIC SCALE.

At first the notes of the chromatic scale should be played on the piano, while the pupil sings the scale, to ensure perfect intonation. These scales, like the preceding ones, should be transposed by semitones, and at first practised very slowly.

32

MINOR SCALES.

These scales are to be transposed in the same way as the others.

EXERCISES FOR FLEXIBILITY.

These exercises should be sung in one breath and should not be attempted until the pupil is capable of so singing them.   They are to be transposed like all the other exercises.

VARIED SCALES.

When the scales can be sung quickly with ease, they should be practised in **various ways**; with accents, dotted notes, staccato, slurred (legato), slurred and staccato, staccato and slurred (*flûtées*), mezzo staccato, syncopated, crescendo and diminuendo, forte and piano.   This exercise is especially adapted for light voices.   Staccato notes are produced by attacking the note rapidly and crisply (by the *coup de glotte*); they should not be practised too long at a time, as the constant repetition of the *coup de glotte* tires the voice.

The mezzo staccato (*notes flûtées*) is a prolonged staccato.

The accented scales are excellent for promoting flexibility.

34

REPEATED NOTES.

In these exercises the repeated note should be slightly aspirated (ha, ha) in order to make it quite clear; but this aspiration should be carefully avoided in the scales and other exercises.

TRIPLETS.

In practising the triplet, the pupil should accent the middle note in order to avoid inequality; the general tendency is to make the first a dotted note.

E. & S. 2328.

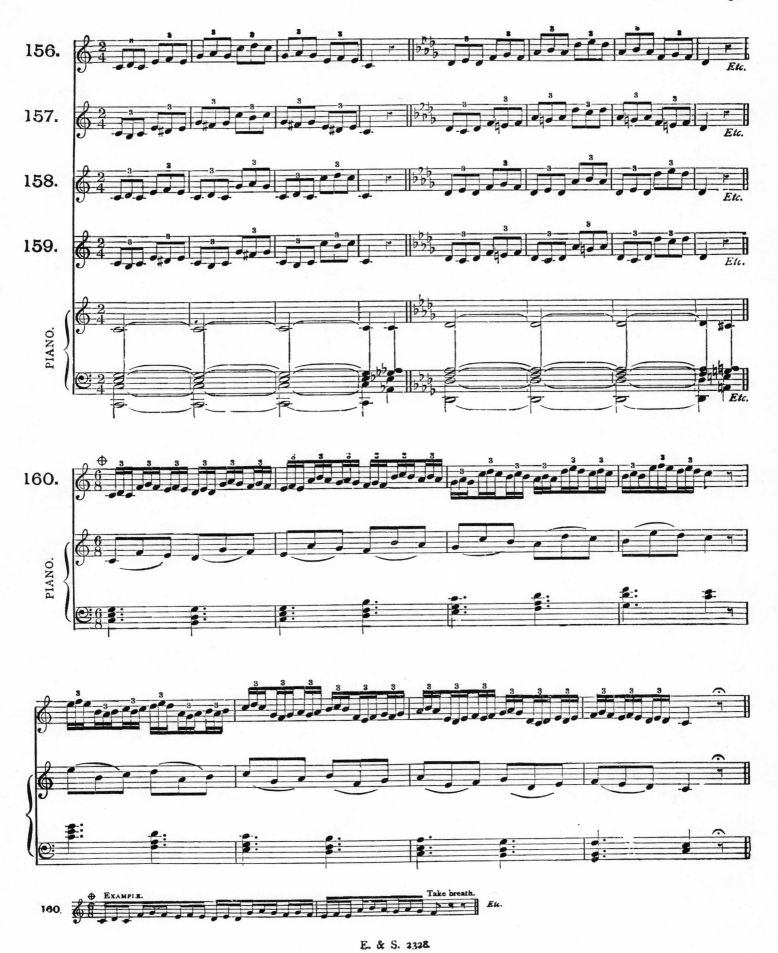

36

161.

162.

PIANO.

ARPEGGI.

Arpeggi should be sung quite evenly, avoiding, above all, any increase of power in the higher notes.

The pupil should pass with precision from one note to another, not by detaching them, **but by** lightly joining them.

38

MESSA DI VOCE (Swelled Sounds).

The *messa di voce* should not be practised until the voice has acquired a certain degree of suppleness and flexibility, and should never be attempted by beginners.

APPOGGIATURA.

The appoggiatura is the easiest of all vocal ornaments. It is, as its Italian name implies, a note on which the voice leans, before passing on to the real note of the chord. The appoggiatura is generally a note foreign to the harmony; it may be above or below the note of the chord and its duration is very variable.

In duple time it takes half the value of the note it precedes, and in triple time it takes two thirds of the value of the principal note. Its duration generally depends upon the character of the phrase.

The appoggiatura may be at any interval from a semitone upwards.

ACCIACCATURA (crushed note).

The acciaccatura is a rapid little note which precedes by a tone or a semitone a second note which is longer.

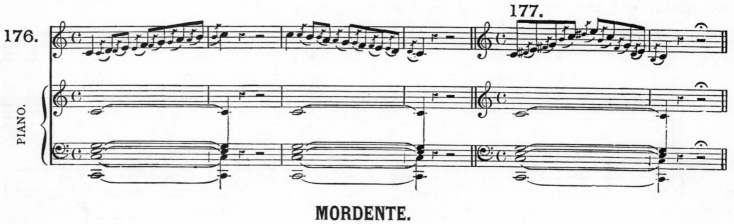

MORDENTE.

The mordente consists of a group of two or three notes preceding the melodic note. This group should be executed rapidly, although at first it should be practised slowly, so as to make each note distinct.

THE TURN.

The turn (gruppetto) is a group of two, three, or four notes, which do not form part of the melody. It consists of a combination of the upper and lower appoggiatura, with the principal note.

42

THE SHAKE (Trill).

The shake is a regular oscillation of the larynx. It is a rapid alternation of two notes a tone or a semitone (a major or minor second) apart. The only way to acquire a good shake is by practising in strict time with the same number of notes to each beat. At first it should be practised slowly, but as the voice gains suppleness the speed may be increased in proportion. To avoid fatigue, female voices should commence practising the shake in the *medium register*.

These exercises, like the others, should be transposed chromatically.

THE WAY TO PRACTISE THE SHAKE.

DIFFERENT ENDINGS OF THE SHAKE.

SCALE OF SHAKES.

SHAKES BY THIRDS.

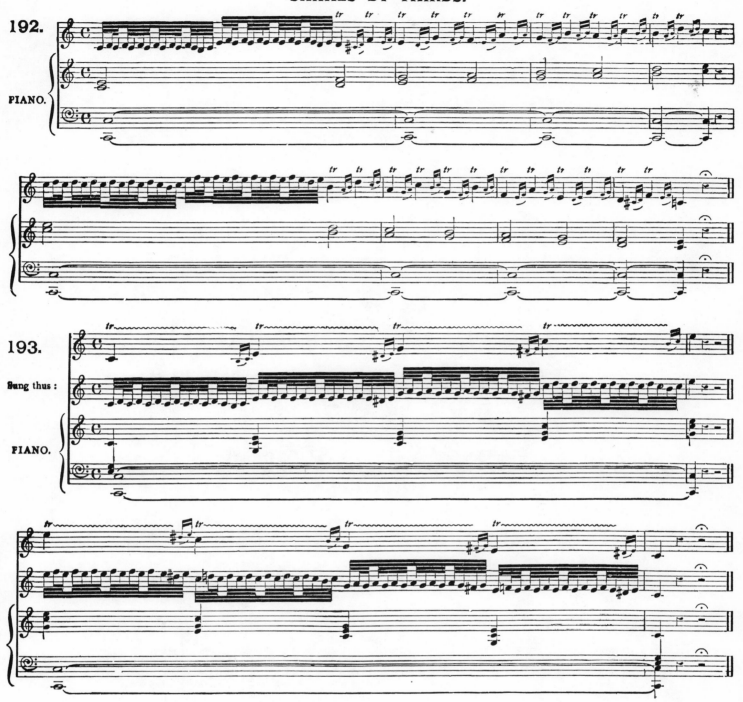

EXERCISE
to facilitate the practice of the shake for voices which are lacking in suppleness.

L. & S. 2328.   END OF THE FIRST PART.

THE MARCHESI VOCAL METHOD.

SECOND PART.

DEVELOPMENT OF THE EXERCISES IN THE FORM OF VOCALISES.

ATTACK.

PORTAMENTO.

PORTAMENTO.

PORTAMENTO.

PORTAMENTO.

50

E. & S. 2328.

PORTAMENTO.

PORTAMENTO.

7.
VOICE.

PIANO.

Andante.

p

SOSTENUTO.

53

8.
VOICE.

PIANO.

E. & S. 2320.

54

SOSTENUTO.

DIATONIC SCALE.

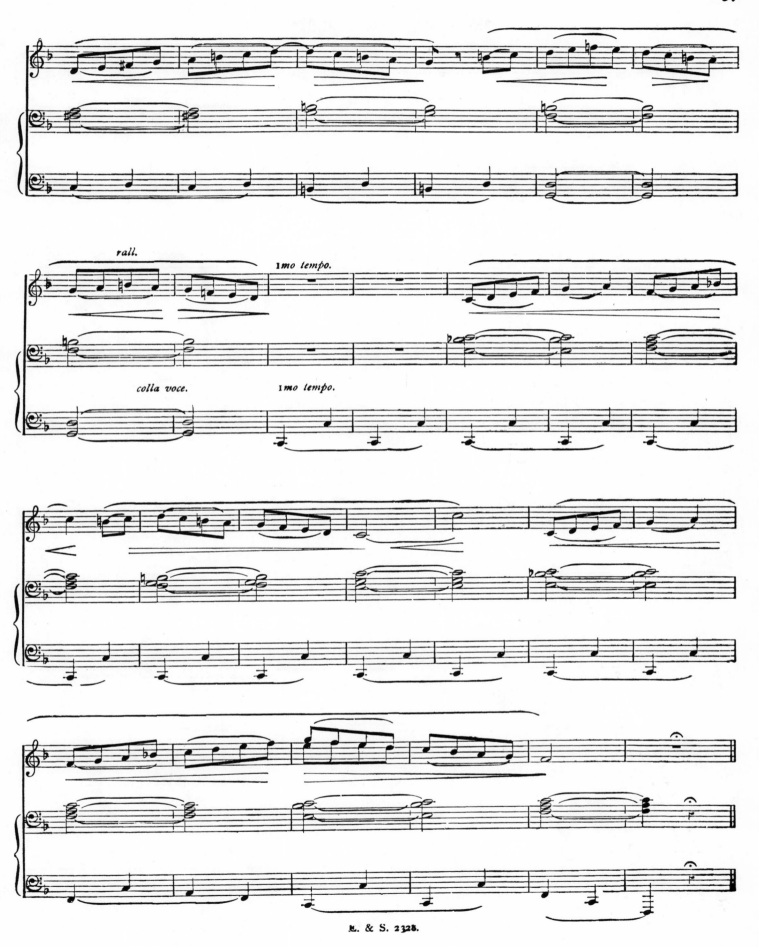

rall. 1mo tempo.

colla voce. 1mo tempo.

DIATONIC SCALE.

DIATONIC SCALE.

DIATONIC SCALE.

DIATONIC SCALE.

DIATONIC SCALE.

DIATONIC SCALE.

DIATONIC SCALE.

rall.   1mo tempo.

colla voce.   1mo tempo.

E. & S. 2324.

DIATONIC SCALE.

72

DIATONIC SCALE.

DOTTED DIATONIC SCALE.

DOTTED DIATONIC SCALE.

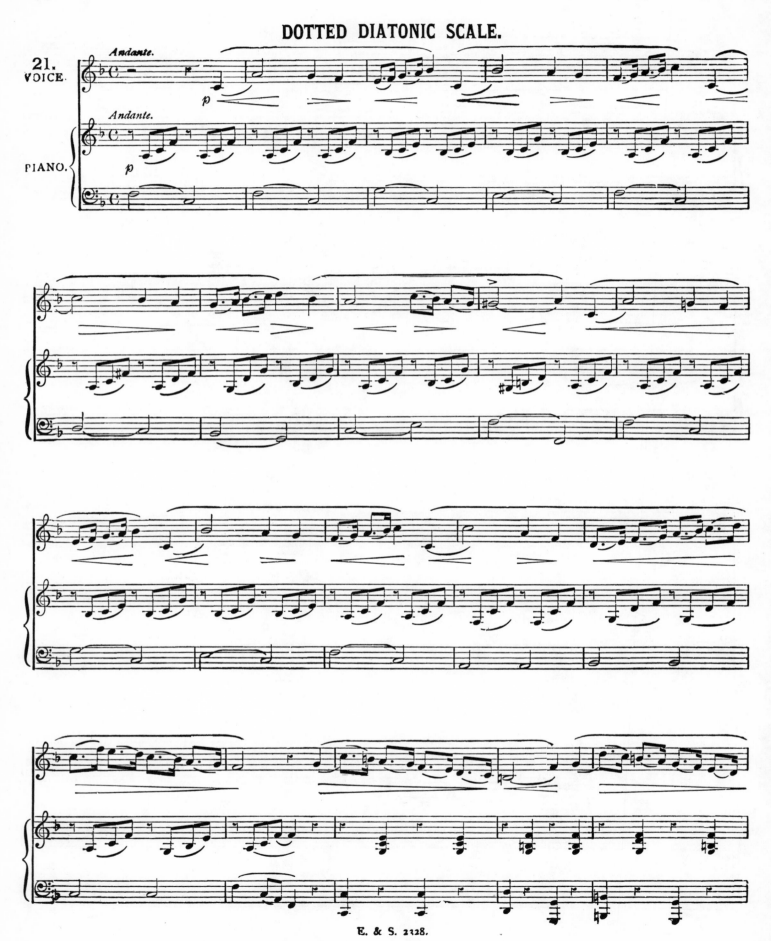

MINOR SCALE.

MAJOR AND MINOR SCALES ALTERNATING.

E. & S. 2328.

MAJOR AND MINOR SCALES ALTERNATING.

E. & S. 2328.

MAJOR AND MINOR SCALES ALTERNATING.

CHROMATIC SCALE.

87

CHROMATIC SCALE.

REPEATED NOTES.

E. & S. 2328.

TRIPLETS.

ARPEGGI.

96

APPOGGIATURA AND ACCIACCATURA (Grace Notes).

E. & S. 2328.

MORDENTE AND TURNS.

SYNCOPATION.

LONG INTERVALS.

STACCATO, MEZZO-STACCATO, AND ACCENTED NOTES.

SHAKES.

108

E. & S. 2328.